More Power through the Fruit of the Holy Spirit

A Short Bible Study

Guadalupe C. Casillas

MORE POWER THROUGH THE FRUIT OF THE HOLY SPIRIT

Copyright © 2024 by Guadalupe C. Casillas.

All rights reserved. No part of this publication may be reproduced or distributed in any form or by any means, electronic or mechanical, without prior written permission from the author.

Requests for permission to make copies of any part of this work should be emailed to the author (isaboutJesus@gmail.com), subject line "permissions." The author hereby grants permission to reviewers to quote up to 100 words from up to three chapters in their reviews, and requests that hyperlinks to said reviews be emailed to the address above.

ISBN 13: 978-1-7334610-4-7

Library of Congress Control Number: 2024910001

Copies of this book are available at online retailers.

For signed copies of this book please contact:
Guadalupe C. Casillas
isaboutJesus@gmail.com
www.GuadalupeCCasillas.com

Cover Art: Red grape on the vine in the sunrise: © 2017, Gelner Tivadar, Stock photo ID:852641414

Book edited by Lawrence Dávila and Eduardo D. Casillas.

Unless otherwise noted, all Scripture quotations are taken from the Holy Bible, New International Version®, NIV® Copyright © 1973, 1978, 1984, 2011 by Biblica, Inc.® Used by permission. All rights reserved.

Scripture quotations marked NLT are taken from the Holy Bible. New Living Translation copyright © 1996, 2004, 2007, 2013 by Tyndale House Foundation. Used by permission of Tyndale House Publishers Inc., Carol Stream, Illinois 60188. All rights reserved.

Printed in United States of America

Dedicated to my Great Counselor, the precious Holy Spirit

Contents

Note to Leaders 2
Bible Study Guidelines 3
Introduction .4
The Fruit of the Holy Spirit 6
Lesson One ~ Love 11
Lesson Two ~ Joy 17
Lesson Three ~ Peace 24
Lesson Four ~ Patience 30
Lesson Five ~ Kindness 36
Lesson Six ~ Goodness 41
Lesson Seven ~ Faithfulness 46
Lesson Eight ~ Gentleness 51
Lesson Nine ~ Self-Control 55
Acknowledgments 62
About the Author 64

Note to Leaders

Thank you for making yourself available to God by facilitating this study. I am praying for you!

If you choose to lead this study during the summer months, I suggest you select a regular meeting place, so people will know where the study will be each week. Make sure the participants bring their Bible, this study workbook, a regular dictionary, and a pen.

This study is simple, just take turns reading the Bible passages and discussing the related questions during your group meeting. There is no homework involved. Open the study with a prayer and allow at least fifteen minutes at closing for prayer requests. Go at your own pace and enjoy your time together. There is more information contained in the Guidelines and Introduction sections.

Introduce yourselves and reintroduce each other when a new person joins the study. You could say your name, where you were born, if you're single or married, and whether you have children and grandchildren. It's crucial to feel comfortable with the people in your group and to develop friendships.

You may also plan a couple of lunch outings or picnics with your group. Make it fun!

I pray this easy and light study will be of many blessings to you and your group.

Bible Study Guidelines

Leaders, please read aloud to your group.

- All sensitive information and prayer requests are confidential.
- Feel free to ask questions. We're here to learn from each other and to grow spiritually from the Word of God.
- Whenever in doubt about any Scripture or things said in your study, I recommend you check with God in prayer, and seek advice from your church leaders and Christian mentors.
- Be brief and specific when requesting prayer, preferably in one or two sentences. This will allow plenty of time to pray for each need. Refrain from giving unsolicited advice and respect the privacy of the person requesting prayer.
- Since we're from various backgrounds and different churches, we'll respect each other's opinions and beliefs, using the Bible as our ultimate reference of truth. We also don't discuss politics during Bible study.
- We'll leave right after the Bible study in order not to impose on our host. If you'd like to visit with someone from your group after the study, you can either talk in your car or go out for coffee.

I pray you will grow closer and deeper in your relationship with Jesus. May God pour His blessings on you and your family!

In His Love,
Guadalupe

Introduction

This is a short and simple Bible study that can be done at any time of the year, though it was tailored to fit the summer months when most Bible study groups go on break, or for people who want to do a light study. Each chapter focuses on a different topic and there is no assigned homework. This approach makes it convenient for families that travel during the summer, or are busy with family activities.

When I was new to Bible studies, our leader encouraged the group to take part in a short summer Bible study, so that we could stay in the Word during that period. I decided not to engage in a group as I wanted some leisure time to myself. Little did I know that my "leisure time," would leave me feeling spiritually dry. I lacked the discipline to read the Bible on my own. Something was missing in my life, but I couldn't put my finger on it. Not being involved in any type of small groups for three months was a spiritual desert for me.

My spiritual oasis came in the Fall when the regular Bible studies resumed at my church. After my first time back, I realized that my soul was in desperate need of Living Water. Now I make it a point to be involved in a flexible summer study, or at least read a short devotional during my daily quiet time at home. I do it because I know my soul needs it.

This special leisure time with God gives me the strength to cope with the challenges that might come up during the day, as well as to have more joy and peace in my heart.

Some church-based Bible studies take a break during the summer months and resume when the children are back in school. I made it a practice to lead a short Bible study book around mid-July, where the participants were free to show up whenever they were available. It was on a drop-in basis and there was no need to call ahead when they couldn't attend. If they were only able to make it to a couple of the sessions, it was better than none.

You are about to see the simplicity of this Bible study book and at the same time learn Scriptures that will empower you greatly to handle the small and big things of life. This is your study so feel free to go at your own pace. If you are doing this with a group, you will have ample time to share your own experiences as I intentionally did not share too much about my personal life, or provided too much commentary as I did in my book titled, *How to Love God with All Your Heart – A Personal Journey and Testimonial Bible Study Guide,* so you could have plenty of time to share your own journey or listen to others share their stories without rushing.

Delight and refresh yourself in this special time with God. May He bless you and empower you as you read His wonderful Word!

The Fruit of the Holy Spirit

The lessons ahead are focused on each fruit of the Holy Spirit, as noted in Galatians 5:22-23, *"But the Holy Spirit produces this kind of fruit in our lives: love, joy, peace, patience, kindness, goodness, faithfulness, gentleness, and self-control. There is no law against these things!"* (NLT)

By studying the Fruit of the Holy Spirit you'll discover how to become and continue to be a fruitful Christian. John 15:5 says, *"I am the vine; you are the branches. If you remain in me and I in you, you will bear much fruit; apart from me you can do nothing."* (NIV)

In order to produce good fruit, we need to remain in the Vine, which is Jesus. God, the Gardener, waters and prunes us to produce good fruit in our lives. He enables us to be fruitful with His strength and power. Our Father wants us to be more and more like Jesus!

Most of us have heard about Jesus, His death on the cross and His glorious resurrection. We have heard God is our Heavenly Father and Creator, who sent His one and only Son to die for us to pay for our sins. But many do not know much about the role of the Holy Spirit. Read the definitions of the words Holy and Spirit according to the Merriam-Webster dictionary © 2004.

Holy: 1. Worthy of absolute devotion 2. sacred 3. having a divine quality.

Holy Spirit: The third person of the Christian Trinity.

Spirit: 1. A life-giving force, soul, 2. Holy Spirit.

Jesus said this about the Holy Spirit in John 16:13-15, *"But when He, the Spirit of truth, comes, He will guide you into all the truth. He will not speak on His own; He will speak only what He hears, and He will tell you what is yet to come. He will glorify me because it is from me that He will receive what He will make known to you. All that belongs to the Father is mine. That is why I said the Spirit will receive from me what He will make known to you."*

"Not only did Jesus give us the gift of salvation, but He left us another precious gift—the Holy Spirit. The Spirit of God living inside of us! Who is the Holy Spirit? He is the third person of the Trinity—the Spirit of God. The day you accept Jesus into your heart, you receive eternal life, and you also obtain a Helper and Counselor to be with you until the end of this age—free of charge. Imagine how much money you would pay a counselor to help you all the days of your life." *(How to Love God with All Your Heart – A Personal Journey & Testimonial Bible Study Guide © 2015)*

What did Jesus say that the Holy Spirit would do in the lives of the believers? We find this in John 14:25-26 NLT, *"I am telling you these things now while I am still with you. But when the Father sends the Advocate as my representative— that is, the Holy Spirit—He will teach you everything and will remind you of everything I have told you."* Jesus also said in John 16:7-8 NLT, *"But in fact, it is best for you that I go away, because if I don't, the Advocate won't come. If I do go away, then I will send Him to you. And when He comes, He will convict the world of its sin, and of God's righteousness, and of the coming judgment."* Yes, He will help us and teach us!

In this study we are going to concentrate on the different types of fruits that the Holy Spirit can produce in the lives of believers. I say believers because those who haven't received Jesus in their hearts have not received His Holy Spirit, as it says in the Bible verses below.

Romans 8:9

You, however, are controlled not by the sinful nature but by the Spirit, if the Spirit of God lives in you. And if anyone does not have the Spirit of Christ, he does not belong to Christ.

Romans 8:11

And if the Spirit of Him who raised Jesus from the dead is living in you, He who raised Christ from the dead will also give life to your mortal bodies through His Spirit, who lives in you.

1 Corinthians 2:14

The man without the Spirit does not accept the things that come from the Spirit of God, for they are foolishness to him, and he cannot understand them, because they are spiritually discerned.

The moment you repent of your sins and ask Jesus to come into your heart as your Lord and Savior, God's Holy Spirit comes to live in you to be your Counselor and Helper forever. Revelation 3:20 says, *"Here I am! I stand at the door and knock. If anyone hears my voice and opens the door, I will come in and eat with that person, and they with me."* The Holy Spirit is the One who makes it possible for us to live a fruitful life.

Before we continue, you can invite Jesus and His Holy Spirit to come into your heart at this very moment by saying:

Lord Jesus, I believe by faith that You are the Son of God. I believe You died on the cross to pay for all my sins and that You rose from the dead. I repent now of all the wrong I've done and invite you to come into my heart to be my Lord and Savior. I receive Your Holy Spirit and Your gift of eternal life. Please help me to follow You and please You all the days of my life. In Your name, Lord Jesus, I pray. Amen.

Welcome to the family of God!!! God loves you so much that He gave you His Holy Spirit to guide you and to help you enjoy your life on this earth. His Holy Spirit will equip you for the journey ahead. He will help you endure all kinds of trials through His mighty power.

If you still have doubts that are preventing you from taking this step of faith, just keep reading and discovering what the Bible says about making this great decision. It is important to find out, little by little, what God has prepared for you.

As we all know, a fruit is a byproduct of a healthy and nourished tree. I love the comparison about the man or woman who delights in God's law and His wonderful promises to us. If we delight in the law of the Lord, we will yield much fruit.

Psalm 1:1-3 describes a man who delights in the law of the Lord:

Blessed is the one who does not walk in step with the wicked or stand in the way that sinners take or sit in the company of mockers, but whose delight is in the law of the LORD, and who meditates on His law day and night. That person is like a tree planted by streams of water, which yields its fruit in season and whose leaf does not wither—whatever they do prospers.

Prayer:

Thank you Heavenly Father, for the precious gift of your Holy Spirit who is with us forever. Thank you for not leaving us alone. We praise You for always giving us Your Spirit and Your counsel. Help us to tap into Your vast love and power all the days of our lives. In Jesus' name, amen.

LESSON ONE ~ *Love*

1. Describe in your own words the meaning of the word, *love*.

2. What is the dictionary's definition of *love*?

3. What is *love* according to the Bible?
   Read 1 Corinthians 13:4-7, 13, and 1 John 4:10.

Amazing love! The Bible also tells us that God is love. We find this fact in 1 John 4:8, "But anyone who does not love does not know God, for God is love." (NLT)

4. What is unconditional love?
   Read John 3:16, Romans 5:8, and Romans 11:6.

5. Do you love yourself? Where does your self-esteem come from? Who are you according to the following Scriptures? Read Psalm 139:14, Romans 8:16, and Ephesians 2:4-7.

6. How are we to love God according to Matthew 22:37.

Do you already love God with all your heart? Do you love Him more than your spouse, your children, grandchildren, parents, or friends? It's okay if you are not there yet. Loving God is a process that starts when you begin to spend more time with Him. If you want to love God more, I recommend my book, *How to Love God with All Your Heart – A Personal Journey & Testimonial Bible Study Guide*. You will fall more in love with Jesus and discover His great love for you!

7. How did King David, the poor widow, and the woman who anointed Jesus with perfume, showed their love for God in these passages? Why do you think it's difficult for some people to love God in such a powerful and extravagant manner? Would you give all your love and all you have to the Lord? Read 2 Samuel 6:14-15, Mark 12:41-44, and Mark 14:3-9.

8. How can we learn to love God passionately and without reservations? Read Jeremiah 29:13, and Matthew 7:7-8.

Let God know in your prayers your desire to love Him more. You will be amazed to see how He will do this in your life. This has been my prayer to God for many years: "Lord, please help me to love You more and more each day." Over the years I have grown to love God more and have felt His great love for me. I delight in being spiritually near to Him.

9. How can we love our enemies, the difficult people in our lives, and those who have hurt us?
Read Matthew 5:43-47, and Romans 12:17-21.

10. What was Jesus' attitude on the cross toward His mockers? Read Luke 23:34.

11. What is Paul's advice in Colossians 3:13-14?

Only through the power of God's Holy Spirit can we forgive those who have hurt us. I thank the Lord for teaching me, not long ago, how to pray for my enemies. An enemy according to the dictionary is *someone seeking to injure*. I have experienced personal attacks when people tried to hurt me with hateful words. Those words kept coming into my mind as poison, stirring in me anger and hurt. The enemy wanted to inflict pain on me by keeping me angry and hurt. So I prayed for God to soften my heart. I kept praying throughout the day for the Lord to protect my feelings and emotions. It also helped me to listen to Christian music throughout the day to keep my mind focused on the beauty of Jesus.

The Holy Spirit, my precious Counselor, then led me to pray blessings over the person who had hurt me. When the hurtful words wanted to keep playing on my mind, I followed Jesus' advice to pray for our enemies. I began to pray, "Lord, please bless her." The battle kept raging as the evil words against me were taunting me. Again, I would pray, "Lord, please bless her, she doesn't know You. I pray she will come to know You as her Lord and Savior." I was winning the battle through God's power. The enemy (the devil) didn't want me to continue to pray blessings over her so he finally stopped harassing me in my thoughts. The pain and hurt went away. My battle was not against that person. It was against Satan. Victory was mine in Jesus' name. I no longer see this person, but I don't resent her either and that my friends, is more power—divine power from God's Holy Spirit!

When I first heard that we must love our enemies, I thought how difficult it must be. When I asked the Director of Women's Ministries about this issue, she explained that it wouldn't necessarily be the same type of love one has toward a dear friend. Instead, it is Agape love which is more of a sacrificial type of love. This kind comes from the

Holy Spirit, who helps us forgive and not feel hatred toward someone. When this takes place, the Lord sets us free from the hurt that others have caused us.

12. How can you receive the fruit of love?
    Read Matthew 21:22, and Colossians 4:2.

Simply ask God in prayer to give you this awesome gift. He gave you His Holy Spirit to help you. Just ask and believe.

My prayer for you:

May God fill you with His love and His presence always. May you grow to love Him with all your heart. I pray He enables you to feel His great love for you and helps you to love others through His power and strength. In Jesus' name, amen.

Lesson Two ~ *Joy*

1. Describe in your own words the meaning of the word, *joy*.

2. What is the dictionary's definition of *joy*?

3. Read Acts 16:16-40. How can we have joy during difficult trials? What were Paul and Silas doing in prison around midnight, according to verse 25?

These words jumped off the page for me: "severely beaten" (vs.23) and "singing hymns to God" (vs. 25). In the middle of their terrible physical pain these disciples chose joy and singing. That is power from the Holy Spirit. What an amazing passage! As you read the conclusion, you can see how their beatings and unjust treatments were not in vain. Worshipping the Lord resulted in a great miracle. The violent earthquake made everyone's chains come loose and yet, they chose not to escape. Instead, their powerful witness brought salvation to the guard and his household. Joy, joy, joy—pure joy! Only the power of God's Holy Spirit can do that in our lives.

Faith in God, singing worship songs, prayer, and knowledge of God's Word have given me more joy and peace over the years. They delivered me from depression many years ago. My life began to change when I started to attend Bible Studies. Joy eventually arrived and depression disappeared! Happiness is temporary. Joy comes from God, even in the middle of difficult circumstances.

4. Have you ever burst into a song or have felt immense joy after a terrible emotional beating? What was that like?

LESSON TWO ~ *Joy*

A beating doesn't have to be only physical blows to the body. Our minds can also receive severe verbal beatings which can leave us emotionally wounded. I remember many years ago going through a difficult trial and crying out to God. After I got up from my knees, the Lord had comforted me. At the end of my prayer, the Lord assured me that everything was going to be alright. That's when I turned my Christian music louder and began to sing praises to God and danced out of pure joy! The Holy Spirit allows us to sing and dance joyfully as we go through painful circumstances. He lovingly and powerfully does that in our lives. Seek His caring help instead of allowing worry and desperation to cloud your mind and consume your heart. The Lord will restore your joy as He did for His disciples in jail.

The knowledge that this world is not my home and the assurance of a blessed future with God, has allowed me to keep the joy and peace that God so freely loves to give.

5. What would be the opposite of *joy*?

6. What is the dictionary's definition of the word, *depress*.

7. How can we combat depression?
   Read 1 Thessalonians 5:16-18.

I suffered from depression in my early twenties and even questioned God's goodness. I went to see my doctor and explained to him that my symptoms of sadness and low self-esteem were more severe during my pre-menstrual cycle. He was ready to prescribe me some anti-depressants, but I immediately replied, "Doctor wait, give me two weeks and if my condition doesn't improve then I'll start taking them." During that time, I was invited to attend my first Bible Study. Over the following weeks, little by little, I experienced a joy so profound that I didn't need to pick up my prescription. Hallelujah!

In some specific cases, people do need to take anti-depressants and they should follow their doctor's orders. In my case, I found the peace and joy I was looking for as I read the Bible, had conversations with God in prayer, and praised Him more often.

May you be strong in the Lord. Have faith in our Savior and keep on praying!

LESSON TWO ~ *Joy*

8. Do you feel emotionally low or inferior at times? For the biblical truth of who exactly God says that you are, read 1 Peter 2:9 and 1 John 3:1. How does it make you feel to know that the Creator of the Universe is your Father?

You are royalty because your Heavenly Father is the King of Kings. I clearly remember when I first read this passage in the Bible. As soon as I saw my husband at home, I told him I was royalty and had "Royal blood running through my veins." He laughed. I said, "It's true, our Heavenly Father is the King of Kings!" So, no matter what others may think of your physical appearance, your job or your possessions, remember that if you belong to God, you are already His prince or princess. You have a rich inheritance. Your Heavenly Father loves you so much that He allowed His Son to die for you, so you could spend eternity with Him enjoying everything He has prepared for you.

9. What was King David's prayer request?
Read Psalm 5:11-12.

10. Read Psalm 51:12. What did David ask God to do for him?

To restore to him the joy of his salvation. Knowing this important truth has increased my joy over the years. The joy of my salvation is secured. Christ died for me to give me eternal life. When all is said and done that is the only thing that will matter, my salvation in Christ Jesus!

11. Paul prayed for the believers to be filled with joy in Romans 15:13. What's the requirement and by whose power? Fill in the blanks below.

May the God of hope fill you with all joy and peace as you _____ in Him, so that you may overflow with _____ by the power of the _____ _____. (Romans 15:13 NIV)

I echo Paul's prayer for each one of you "May the God of hope fill you with all joy and peace as you trust in Him, so that you may overflow with hope by the power of the Holy Spirit."

God doesn't want us to be filled with despair, hopelessness, and sadness. He wants us to be filled with hope, joy, and peace through the empowerment of His Holy Spirit.

LESSON TWO ~ *Joy*

12. What are we called to do according to John 15:9-12 and Philippians 4:4?

The Holy Spirit of God is the One who produces the fruit of joy in our lives. Ask God to help you trust in Him. Give your cares and worries to God and leave them with Him. I used to give my cares and worries to God in prayer but minutes later I would take them back. Worry and despair would come back also, that is why I said, "Leave them with Him." Pray that God will increase your faith and trust in Him. Rest in His precious time. He will take care of all your needs, as He promised.

My prayer for you:

Thank you, dear Holy Spirit, for the gift of joy! I pray You will develop this precious gift in the person reading this book right now. Infuse him or her with more of your Spirit and may all the darkness of hopelessness and depression leave in Jesus' name. Fill them abundantly with Your joy. In Your precious name, I pray, amen.

Lesson Three ~ *Peace*

1. Describe in your own words the meaning of the word, *peace*.

2. What is the dictionary's definition of *peace*?

3. How do you find peace when you're having a difficult day?

I don't walk to Jesus with my problems and petitions, I run to Him! As soon as the situation presents itself, I go to my Heavenly Father and give the issue over to Him. It's incredible how I can feel His peace right away. It was a big waste of time and energy to worry about my problems. Nowadays, I do not hesitate to ask God for His loving favor and help. He sometimes handles my problem so quickly that I don't even have to lift a finger. Jesus has made my problems disappear countless times!

Even when our situation does not change, we can experience His wonderful peace during that time. We can also ask God for wisdom in how to manage our problems. We also need to be willing to accept that God is sovereign and sometimes He allows certain circumstances to make us stronger during those trials.

4. How can we protect our minds from negative thoughts that threaten to rob our peace? Read Romans 8:6.

I protect my peace by asking the Holy Spirit to control my mind and by being obedient to Him. Panic attacks still knock at my door from time to time. As soon as I begin to feel anxious, I come to the Lord in prayer. He reminds me that who the Son sets free is free indeed. (John 8:36)

At that moment I thank the Lord that I'm free by the blood of Jesus and say, "I know I'm free and that I am healed in the name of the Father, the Son and the Holy Spirit." At that moment I begin to feel His peace, which transcends all understanding, guarding my heart and my mind in Christ Jesus as it says in Philippians 4:6-7, one of my favorite Bible verses.

5. Read Matthew 8:23-27. Discuss Jesus' words to his disciples, "You of little faith, why are you so afraid?" How can those words apply to us, too?

The disciples were afraid. They didn't have control over the situation. Jesus then calmed the storm just by speaking to it. Years ago, I literally saw God stop a storm right after I prayed and said amen. My two young sons and I were in the car when suddenly, a heavy rainstorm came down on the freeway, making it hard to see all around me.

Carefully and prayerfully, I pulled to the side of the road. I then began to pray aloud, "Dear God please stop the rain so we can get back on the road. As soon as I said, "Amen," the storm stopped completely, no trickling water, no drizzle, it was gone in a second. My son, Ed, who was in the passenger seat looked at me astonished and then exclaimed, "Yay, God!" We proceeded to give thanks. Still filled with wonder by the mighty power of God, we went back on the road this time singing praises to Him. This powerful experience taught me that Jesus can just say to the storm, "Stop" and it obeys Him at once.

6. What is fear? Share a time when you were afraid, in the middle of a crisis, and Jesus calmed you down with His peace.

7. Name some of the common fears we face in this world.

8. Why if we believe God is our Father, do we sometimes continue to be afraid?

9. How can we combat a spirit of fear?
   Read Romans 8:15, and 2 Timothy 1:7.

10. How do we obtain peace and who gives it to us?
    Read Psalm 29:11, and Philippians 4:6-9.

11. How do you keep peace and harmony in your home, workplace, church, etc.?

12. What thought, or Scripture verse brings you peace of mind?

My prayer for you:

May His peace flow abundantly over you as you trust in Him. May He remind you of all the goodness and blessings He has brought into your life. In Jesus' name, amen.

Optional:

During the week, make a list of the things for which you are thankful. Start with your spiritual blessings and then physical and material blessings. Your list of blessings will uplift you, comfort you, and remind you that God is good and faithful all the time!

Lesson Four ~ *Patience*

1. Describe in your own words the meaning of the word, *patience*.

2. What is the dictionary's definition of *patience*?

3. Read James 1:2-4 and share your thoughts from these verses.

LESSON FOUR ~ *Patience*

4. What is perseverance? Read James 5:7-11.

5. What type of situations cause you to become impatient?

6. What do you think causes you to be impatient or to become irritated? Read Romans 7:18.

7. How can we learn to be patient with the people around us? Read Proverbs 19:11, and Proverbs 25:15.

The Lord has helped me to control my temper and to not blurt things out when I'm upset. Sometimes, the Holy Spirit says to me in my thoughts, "Bite your tongue, Guadalupe" which works every time. He has shown me to know what to say and what not to say, as well as waiting for the right time to say it.

The Bible verses above have given me wisdom to better manage those situations. With kind and soft words, or keeping quiet, I have avoided losing my temper. It requires the help of the Holy Spirit to not say the first thing that comes to mind. Satan likes to cause strife and divisions in relationships. It is better to be sensible and patient. When I find myself in the middle of an intense argument, I immediately say a silent prayer in my head to ask God to help me control myself. Remember wisdom comes from the Lord and "Soft speech can break bones," and that it is better to "Overlook wrongs." Power, remember—more power through the Fruit of His Holy Spirit!

Lesson Four ~ Patience

8. The disciples were persecuted and suffered harsh conditions and yet they had joy, peace, and perseverance. Most of us don't face the kind of persecutions that they did, such as beatings and death, but we can be persecuted in different ways. What types of suffering or negative experiences have you had because of your faith in Jesus? Have you been mocked or made fun of? How did you respond?

Jesus told us in John 15:18, "If the world hates you, keep in mind that it hated me first."

9. How can we learn to be bold and stand up for our beliefs, instead of losing patience and becoming frustrated or angry? Read Acts 4:29-31.

10. A good example of a man of patience and great perseverance, who suffered many trials, was Job. He was a man who loved the Lord. He didn't curse God despite his many losses. Read Job 1:20-22 and share your thoughts.

11. How did God reward Job for his perseverance? Read Job 42:12-13.

Job was a great man of faith. He left us a notable example of patience, integrity, and perseverance. I admire his love and faithfulness toward our Lord. It is easy to praise God when things are going well in our lives, but when trials and hardships come our way, our faith is tested. Let us be like Job and may God give us the wisdom and strength to say, "...I came naked from my mother's womb, and I will be naked when I leave. The Lord gave me what I had, and the Lord has taken it away. Praise the name of the Lord!" (Job 1:21 NLT)

12. How are we to clothe ourselves? Read Colossians 3:12.

Developing patience can be as simple as asking the Holy Spirit to provide it for us. Nowadays I say, "Lord, please give me patience, in Jesus' name. Amen." I take a deep breath and let God take care of my problems. For example, if I'm stuck waiting in traffic and the situation is out of my control, I just observe the beautiful clouds and enjoy my surroundings. I also practice leaving the house early to avoid being pressed for time while driving. This allows me to be more relaxed during traffic, and to feel less anxious when unexpected delays arise.

When life situations present an obstacle in my calendar, instead of losing my peace and becoming frustrated, I now cheerfully say, "Okay Lord, my plans have changed, so what are we doing today?" His plans are always better than mine.

My prayer for you:

May the Lord give you this fruit of His Holy Spirit. May He help you be patient with yourself and with others for your own well-being. In Jesus' name, I pray, amen!

Lesson Five ~ *Kindness*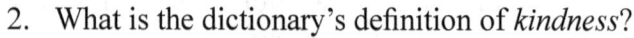

1. Describe in your own words the meaning of the word, *kindness*.

2. What is the dictionary's definition of *kindness*?

3. What is the opposite of *kindness*?

4. Define the word, *rude*.

5. How does it make you feel when you see someone being rude? Give an example.

6. How do you react when you see someone showing kindness? Share an example.

7. How are we to treat one another? Read Ephesians 4:32.

8. What did Jesus say in Matthew 5:43-48?

9. Read John 15:1-5, and 1 Corinthians 13:4. How can we be kind to an unkind person?

John 4:8 tells us that, "God is love," and 1 Corinthians 13:4 says that "Love is patient and love is kind". Consequently, God is patient and God is kind. Apart from the Vine which is Jesus, we can do nothing. Only by asking the Holy Spirit to produce the fruit of kindness in us, we can then be kind to the unkind.

I tried so hard in the past, on my own strength, to be kind to difficult people and found that it is extremely hard. God has taught me that all I need to do is ask Him to help me be kind and patient in those situations. When we remain attached to the Vine we will become more like Him. He enables us to produce good fruit!

10. What does Proverbs 11:16-17 says about kind people?

LESSON FIVE ~ *Kindness*

11. Read Titus 3:4-7. How did Jesus reveal His kindness to us? Make a list of everything He lovingly did for us.

I thank the Lord so much for His love and kindness to us. Only by the power of His Holy Spirit can we learn to be kind and loving to others and even to ourselves. I say to ourselves because God wants us to be kind and loving to our own minds and bodies.

Some people have a challenging time being kind to themselves. Some are workaholics or alcoholics. Others, unfortunately, try to pacify their minds by using chemical substances like drugs, and even excessive food addictions, damaging their bodies in the process.

Be kind to your mind and your body by the simple act of resting and not feeling guilty about it. Sometimes we buy into the mentality that resting is laziness. Eventually, our own bodies will take a toll and suffer from various illnesses due to stress.

If God has shown you kindness by saving you, giving you a new birth and new life, also ask Him to help you receive His great kindness and to be able to enjoy it. From His marvelous kindness to us, we can also extend His kindness to others and be patient with them. It will give you a rewarding feeling to be kind—He designed you that way!

12. Write Jeremiah 31:3 from the New International Version here. How can you thank God for His love and kindness to you?

My prayer for you:

May the Lord help you by the power of His Holy Spirit, to be kind to yourself and to others. I pray He will make you aware of His great presence and kindness to you. In Jesus' name, amen.

Lesson Six ~ *Goodness*

1. Describe in your own words the meaning of the word, *goodness*.

2. What is the dictionary's definition of *goodness*?

3. When did evil enter humanity? Read Genesis 2:16-17 and Genesis 3:4-6.

4. How did God protect Adam and Eve even after they sinned against Him? Read Genesis 3:21-23.

5. Describe the character of God according to the following verses: Psalm 33:5, Psalm 118:1, and Psalm 145:9.

6. Why did Jesus say that He is the Good Shepherd? Read John 10:11-18.

7. Why do we struggle with the desires of the flesh? Read Romans 7:18-19.

8. How can we overcome evil and do what we are called to do? Read Ephesians 5:1-20 and share your thoughts.

All these divine instructions are for our own benefit. Apart from God, we can make a mess out of our lives. Please carefully heed these warnings and loving advice. Verse seventeen says, "Don't act thoughtlessly, but understand what the Lord wants you to do." Let us think carefully about our decisions and actions, always checking with God our Father in prayer to know what He wants us to do. The Lord will always give us the best advice and path to take.

Years ago, I accidentally got out on the wrong exit on the freeway. I didn't realize it until I looked around the empty fields on both sides of the freeway and nothing looked familiar. Approaching a fork in the road I didn't know whether to turn right or left. There were no gas stations, buildings, or homes where I could find someone to ask for directions. Immediately I said a quick prayer, "Lord, please help me. Which way do I go?" It was not an audible voice, but I instinctively turned left. A few yards ahead I saw an entrance to a freeway, but still didn't know where it would lead me. Right before fully merging on that freeway I spotted a police car pulled on the side of the road. Slowly, I parked behind him since he was the only human being available to ask around.

I exited my vehicle slowly and carefully so I wouldn't startle the police officer and began to ask if this freeway would lead me to my destination. He smiled and confirmed that I was on the right path. I said, "You are an angel sent by God. I prayed for the Lord to help me find the right way and you just happened to be here, thank you!" God is good and always willing to help us in our time of need, and point us to the right direction.

9. How can we make the devil flee? Read James 4:7 in the New International Version.

As you see in this verse it says, "Resist the devil and he will flee from you," but the most important part is the beginning of this verse, "Submit yourselves, then, to God." The only way you can be victorious against the evil plans of the enemy is to start with God!

10. Read Ephesians 2:8-10 (NIV). Are we saved just by being good? According to verse ten, what did God create us for? Please explain.

11. Read Psalm 23:6 and write it down. You may also want to write it on a 3x5 card and post it on your refrigerator to remind yourself of the goodness of the Lord.

The key word here is, "Surely!" It is a sure deal that as we follow the Lord, His goodness will follow us all the days of our lives.

12. Read Psalm 103 to learn more about God's goodness. Make a list of all of God's benefits for you!

A benefit according to the Merriam-Webster's dictionary is: Something that produces good or helpful results or effects or that promotes well-being: advantage.

This is huge! Check the following verses below and meditate on them:

He forgives all my sins and heals all my diseases. He redeems me from death and crowns me with love and tender mercies. He fills my life with good things. My youth is renewed like the eagle's! (Psalm 103:3-5 NLT)

I think the only logical response to these Bible verses is immense gratitude to our good and compassionate Lord.

My prayer for you:

May the Lord bless you and remind you of His goodness toward you. May your knowledge of His love and goodness increase as you continue to seek Him. In Jesus' name, amen.

Lesson Seven ~ *Faithfulness*

1. Describe in your own words the meaning of the word, *faithfulness*.

2. What is the dictionary's definition of *faithfulness*?

3. Who initiates our faith according to Hebrews 12:2?

4. What will you receive when you do good according to Proverbs 14:22?

LESSON SEVEN ~ *Faithfulness*

5. What does the Bible say about God's faithfulness? Read 2 Timothy 2:13.

6. Read Lamentations 3:22-23. What does it reveal about God's faithfulness toward you?

7. What does Numbers 23:19 say about God? How does it make you feel to know that God will never lie to you?

I am so glad that God does not lie. I can always trust Him. He is forever faithful and true!

8. Share an experience when God demonstrated His faithfulness to you.

9. Explain God's faithfulness according to Psalm 36:5.

Let's study in the book of Genesis on the faithfulness of God toward Abraham. In Genesis 12:1-4 we read that God had promised Abram, whose name the Lord would later change to Abraham, that He would make him into a great nation, even though his wife Sarah was barren.

The Lord had said to Abram, "Leave your native country, your relatives, and your father's family, and go to the land that I will show you. I will make you into a great nation. I will bless you and make you famous, and you will be a blessing to others. I will bless those who bless you and curse those who treat you with contempt. All the families on earth will be blessed through you." So Abram departed as the Lord had instructed, and Lot went with him. Abram was seventy-five years old when he left Harran. (Genesis 12:1-4 NLT)

10. What was God's promise to Abraham in Genesis 15:1-6?

11. Read Genesis 21:1-5. Did God keep his promise to Abraham?

It took twenty-five years for God to fulfill His promise to Abraham, and yet he never doubted the Lord. He believed God! God is never late to His promises. When I first read this story in the Bible, it surprised me that the Lord took so long to fulfill His promise. It taught me that God's timing is not my timing. He is always in control and will follow through with His promises.

As a newlywed I grew weary and tired of asking God that my husband one day would come back to church with me. I prayed for two years and after not receiving an answer, I doubted God's goodness, and even doubted His existence.

I thought, "I'm asking for something good here, I'm not asking for riches or wealth and yet God does not seem to care." I stopped praying and believing. Depression sunk in at the thought that God may not exist, and I even questioned my purpose for living. When I was invited to attend a Bible study my life began to change. My small group was a safe place where I could ask the deep questions of life. Reading the Bible allowed me to get to know God better and to accept His perfect will and timing for my life.

At the end of twenty-two years of praying for my husband, he finally came to church with me. His faith in God was also renewed. He said that what had made an impact in his life was seeing my faithfulness to God during all those years. God was faithful to us and He made something beautiful of our lives!

12. Read Genesis 22:1-18. What can we learn from Abraham's faithfulness to God in this passage? How can this test apply to you as well?

My prayer for you:

May the Lord increase your faith and keep you faithful by the power of His Holy Spirit. In Jesus' name, amen.

Lesson Eight ~ *Gentleness*

1. Describe in your own words the meaning of the word, *gentleness*.

2. What is the dictionary's definition of *gentleness*?

3. What is the opposite of being gentle?

4. What can a gentle answer do and what can harsh words do? Read Proverbs 15:1.

5. What are we told to do according to Ephesians 4:2?

6. What are we called to pursue in 1 Timothy 6:11?

7. How are we recommended to talk to non-believers about Christ? Read 1 Peter 3:15-16.

8. How did Jesus describe himself in Matthew 11:29?

9. How is God's wisdom described in these verses? Read James 3:16-18.

10. What is the advice given to wives of non-believers? Read 1 Peter 3:1-4.

I followed this advice from Scripture and it was a great blessing! I used to be angry at Eduardo for not coming to church with me and our two boys. Until I read this passage in one of our Bible studies and my friends explained this verse to me "…Your godly lives will speak to them without any words." From that point on I would leave the house on Sunday mornings and would give my husband a gentle kiss and wished him a good day, as I drove myself and our sons to church, instead of chastising him.

He began to feel remorse being that I remained sweet and caring. When I would return home from church, I noticed that he had been busy all morning vacuuming and doing chores around the house. He would then ask me, "How was church?" "What was the message about?" "Did you have a good time?" My heart was glad to see that my husband was genuinely interested to hear about the morning's message. Eduardo also noticed that I was becoming gentler and sweeter. He liked the quiet spirit the Lord had produced in me and one day he finally decided to start joining us on Sundays! I love how the Word of God is full of wisdom and great advice.

11. What are we to avoid as believers and what does our attitude should be instead? Read Titus 3:1-2.

Remember that gentleness is a fruit of the Holy Spirit. He produces these precious fruits in our lives. We can try being gentle and kind on our own strength, but the difficult part is to do that with those who may not like us very much. That's when we ask God to help us be humble and gentle. He makes our lives easier!

12. Mention a time when you didn't feel like being gentle toward others and how the Holy Spirit helped you.

My prayer for you:

May God's Holy Spirit fill you with all of His gifts. May He give you all good things according to His glorious riches. I pray He will enable you to be gentle and be more like Jesus. In His name, I pray, amen.

Lesson Nine ~ *Self-Control*

1. Describe in your own words the meaning of the word, *self-control*.

2. What is the dictionary's definition of *self-control*?

3. Mention some of the times when the Holy Spirit helped you exercise self-control.

I enjoyed eating sour fruits like green mangos, pineapple, and green apples with salt. Even though the acidity of these fruits caused my teeth to hurt, I couldn't stop eating them.

Over time my two front teeth lost their enamel protection which gave me excruciating pain. My dentist recommended veneers to alleviate my condition. As I laid on the dentist's chair during the procedure, I asked the Lord to please help me stop this terrible habit. My dentist warned me that the new veneers could also be ruined if I continued. This habit of mine was not harmless, it was destructive.

I then thought of people who have other addictions. They know they are hurting their bodies but can't stop. I felt sad for them. My own type of addiction made me more sympathetic to those struggling with theirs. Sometimes, people don't stop their bad habits until it is too late. They ruin their lungs, their liver, their heart and just about any organ that suffers when we abuse sugar, salt, fats, oils, drugs, alcohol, cigarettes, you name it. It doesn't have to be only foods or drugs, it can be a lack of self-control when it comes to anger, verbal abuse, lust, etc. But thanks be to God who can help us by giving us His fruit of self-control when we ask for it. Just keep on asking, His Holy Spirit will enable you to have victory after victory.

The pain was gone with my new veneers protecting my two front teeth. The Lord heard my prayer and helped me stop that destructive habit. I began to enjoy sweet fruits instead and without salt, which lowered my sodium intake. Thank you, Lord!

LESSON NINE ~ *Self-Control*

4. What are some of the signs of people with a lack of self-control? Read Proverbs 29:11.

Wise people hold back their anger. Many relationships are destroyed when people lack self-control and vent their anger. Harsh words are spoken and sometimes feelings are broken beyond repair. Let's avoid the awful power of anger and instead allow the Holy Spirit to teach us to hold back, to be wise, self-controlled, kind, and gentle.

5. What is better than conquering a city?
   Read Proverbs 16:32.

6. How was Joseph able to exercise self-control and flee from temptation? Read Genesis 39:1-12.

He ran away! We are to flee from temptation. Joseph respected his master, but above all else, he didn't want to sin against God. Potiphar's wife was ready to cheat on her husband and she didn't seem to care. Oh, if only all men, and women too, were like Joseph—loyal and faithful. Joseph was human and could have failed, but his closeness to God and eagerness to obey him were stronger.

7. How can we obtain self-control? Read Matthew 21:22 and share a time when prayer has helped you resist temptations in your life.

8. What is the benediction found in Hebrews 13:20-21?

The power of Jesus Christ will produce in us every good thing that is pleasing to Him! God does equip us with all that we need to do His will.

9. Read 1 Corinthians 1:7-9.
   What is the promise found in verse 8?

God is faithful to keep us blameless! Notice here that it is God who will keep us strong and blameless to the end. Our part is to be in partnership with His Son, Jesus.

Over the years, the Lord has helped me develop patience, peace, joy, goodness, kindness, love, gentleness, and faith but the hardest of all still is self-control when it comes to eating sweets. At first, I thought I didn't have self-control at all, but the Holy Spirit reminded me that I do have self-control in other areas of my life. I have self-control in controlling my temper when I'm provoked, buying unnecessary things, and controlling my thought life. The Lord reminded me that He has given me self-control about not overdoing it with sweets, too. Even though this is a weak area in my life, I'm aware of it and the power of God's Holy Spirit has helped me not to develop diabetes, which runs in my family.

At times my blood sugar has been borderline, but as soon as I saw the numbers go up in my lab results, I asked the Lord to help me apply the brakes. Sweet pastries are hard to resist but His Holy Spirit helps me to have the self-control to cut back and make better choices about my health. I don't know what your weaknesses are, but I know God can give you the fruit of self-control to help you be more like Jesus. Be patient and gentle with yourself and continue to ask the Holy Spirit to help you. Don't give up. He will give you the power to resist in the name of Jesus!

10. How are we to live in this present age?
    Read Titus 2:11-14.

11. What did you learn about the Fruit of the Holy Spirit in all of these nine lessons?

12. How can we be fruitful Christians? Read John 15:5.

Notice how all the nine fruits of the Holy Spirit work together. That is why it is called the Fruit of the Holy Spirit, not Fruits (plural) of the Holy Spirit, because they all come from the same Spirit of God. For example, love and patience can go together at the same time, patience and kindness, peace and self-control, goodness and kindness, self-control and gentleness, joy and peace. Out of goodness and love the Lord teaches us to be patient, kind, gentle, peaceful… You get the idea!

Once again, as described in the introduction of this Bible study, we are fruitful and produce good fruits when we are connected to the Vine, which is Jesus. God gave us His Holy Spirit to help us live better lives filled with love, joy, peace, patience, kindness, goodness, faithfulness, gentleness, and self-control.

These divine fruits come from the Holy Spirit. We can try earnestly to obtain these by our own strength and power, but failure is sure to follow. It is easy to be loving and kind to those who are nice. The challenge comes when the people we ought to love are mean and difficult. That is why we pray and ask God to send us His faithful and gracious help. He enables us by the power of His Holy Spirit as we abide in Him.

In conclusion, let this Bible passage speak to your heart about God's spiritual provision for you!

"But blessed is the one who trusts in the Lord, whose confidence is in Him. They will be like a tree planted by the water that sends out its roots by the stream. It does not fear when heat comes; its leaves are always green. It has no worries in a year of drought and never fails to bear fruit." (Jeremiah 17:7-8)

My prayer for you:

May God help you by the power of His Holy Spirit to have the fruit of self-control, as well as His other fruits so you can be strong in your weak areas. May He continue to bless you as you put your trust in Him. May He make you powerful for His glory, in Jesus' name, amen!

Acknowledgments

Thank you, *Escarlet Mar*, for encouraging me to publish this Bible study. I will always remember the day we met for coffee and you said, "One of the reasons I wanted to meet with you is because God wanted me to ask you, when are you going to write your second book?" I was taken aback and replied, "I wrote a short Bible study in 2004, but I was not planning to publish it." I will never forget what you said next, *"Guadalupe, think of all the people that will be blessed through your second book."* The word "blessed" got me! I wrote your words that day on my Bible as a reminder to follow through and publish this study guide. Thank you for allowing God to use you as His precious instrument, and believing that this study would be a blessing to many people. Escarlet, I thank God for you, my beautiful friend. You are a wonderful woman of God!

I'm immensely thankful dear uncle, *Lawrence Dávila*, for your love, time, and effort in editing this study, both in English and Spanish. When I asked the Lord to help me with this endeavor, your name popped into my head during my prayer. No doubt, the Lord wanted us to work together in finishing this project of love. I thank the Lord for your constant support, advice, and wisdom throughout the years. I admire you and love you greatly!

Julie Williams, it has always been a pleasure to work with you as my book designer. Thank you for fitting me into your very busy schedule. I'm so glad you did because you do excellent work!

A big thanks to my beloved husband, *Eduardo D. Casillas*. Thank you, my love, for your many valuable suggestions in the translation, edits, and design of this short Bible study. I would not have been able to do this work without your great help. Never in my dreams, would I have thought God would pair us up not only to be husband and wife, but to also collaborate in this project together for His glory! I love you more than you know, my Prince Charming!

Thank you to all my *Bible study friends* for your wonderful support, encouragement, and friendship. I thank the Lord for bringing all of you into my life. It has been a great blessing to grow in His wisdom during all our Bible Studies. May God richly bless all of you!!!

About the Author

Born in Nicaragua, Guadalupe came to California at the age of sixteen where she met her husband, Eduardo. Currently living in California, they have two sons, Ed and Andrew. Guadalupe has been involved in Bible studies for over thirty-seven years, and leading small groups for the last twenty. The love and mentorship shown to her in her first Bible study group ultimately pointed her to the love of Jesus, which gave her a passion for women's ministries.

Guadalupe has a deep love for Jesus. Through the power of the Holy Spirit she has encouraged those around her to come to know and experience the amazing love of God. For seven years she volunteered with Stonecroft Ministries in Folsom, California, as Hospitality Coordinator, Prayer Coordinator, Chairperson and Bible Study Coordinator. She is currently a Speaker with Stonecroft Ministries, an evangelistic international organization for women.

A good friend suggested she write a Bible study book to share all she has learned in her journey with God. That same week other friends independently suggested she should write as well. After much prayer and discussing it with her husband, she realized it was God's plan for her to write, *"How to Love God with All Your Heart – A Personal Journey and Testimonial Bible Study Guide,"* which she translated into Spanish under the title, *"Cómo amar a Dios con todo tu corazón."* She wrote her first Bible study in 2004, titled

ABOUT THE AUTHOR

"More Power Through the Fruit of the Holy Spirit," to share with her Bible study friends, with no thought of publishing it until now. This Bible study is also available in Spanish under the title, *"Más poder a través del Fruto del Espíritu Santo."*

Guadalupe's prayer is that you will be blessed and encouraged in your journey with God! You can visit her at www.GuadalupeCCasillas.com